Working Scientifically

ASKING QUESTIONS AND FINDING SOLUTIONS

by Riley Flynn

raintree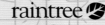

a Capstone company — publishers for children

Raintree is an imprint of Capstone Global Library Limited, a company incorporated in England and Wales having its registered office at 264 Banbury Road, Oxford, OX2 7DY – Registered company number: 6695582

www.raintree.co.uk
myorders@raintree.co.uk

Edited by Anna Butzer
Designed by Sarah Bennett
Picture research by Eric Gohl
Production by Laura Manthe

Printed and bound in China.
ISBN 978 1 4747 2256 8
20 19 18 17 16
10 9 8 7 6 5 4 3 2 1

British Library Cataloguing in Publication Data
A full catalogue record for this book is available from the British Library.

Every effort has been made to contact copyright holders of material reproduced in this book. Any omissions will be rectified in subsequent printings if notice is given to the publisher.

All the internet addresses (URLs) given in this book were valid at the time of going to press. However, due to the dynamic nature of the internet, some addresses may have changed, or sites may have changed or ceased to exist since publication. While the author and publisher regret any inconvenience this may cause readers, no responsibility for any such changes can be accepted by either the author or the publisher.

Acknowledgements
iStockphoto: Pamela Moore, 19; Shutterstock: Annette Shaff, 7, Maxim Khytra, 20, pavla, 17, Photology1971, 11, rck_953, 5, sabzaa, 13, science photo, 15, wavebreakmedia, cover, 9
Design Elements: Shutterstock

Contents

Why we ask questions

In science we ask many questions.

Why is the sky blue? How do birds fly? The questions we ask help us to learn more about the world.

Curiosity is important

A curious person asks questions and looks for answers. Why do dogs pant? Why do rabbits hop? Curiosity helps us to learn.

You throw a paper aeroplane into the air. It crashes to the ground. What went wrong? Are the wings the wrong shape? Asking questions can help to solve a problem.

Observations and answers

To find an answer, you
must first observe the problem.
Your bike isn't working.
It's hard to pedal. Can you
see the problem?

Look closely at your bike.
You see a flat tyre. That's the
problem. How do you solve
the problem? You must
repair the tyre!

Experiments and answers

Scientists use experiments to
help answer questions.
An experiment is a test that
has been carefully planned.
Scientists observe what
happens during an experiment.

Does wood sink in water?
Do rocks float? You can find the
answer by doing an experiment.
With an adult's help, test what
happens by placing these
objects in water.

Look around you. Many things you use began as experiments. People saw problems. They worked to solve them. It may have taken many experiments.

Finding answers

How much of your favourite drink is there in a glass filled with ice?

What you need:

- drinking glass
- water
- 475 millilitre measuring jug, marked with millilitres
- small building blocks
- an adult to help you

What to do:

1. Fill the drinking glass with water. Then pour the water into the measuring jug.

2. Make a note of the measurement in millilitres. Empty the jug.

3. Carefully place the small blocks in the bottom of the drinking glass. These represent ice cubes.

4. Fill the glass with water. Then pour the water into the measuring jug.

5. Remove the blocks.

6. Make a note of the measurement in millilitres.

7. Find the difference between the two measurements. Use subtraction.

Glossary

curious eager to explore and learn about new things

experiment scientific test to find out how something works

observe watch someone or something closely in order to learn about it

problem something that raises questions

repair fix or mend

solve find the answer to a problem

Read more

The Big Book of Science: Things to Make and Do (Usborne Activities), Rebecca Gilpin (Usborne Publishing, 2012)

Experiments with Forces (Read and Experiment), Isabel Thomas (Raintree, 2015)

Websites

www.bbc.co.uk/bitesize/ks1/science
Enjoy some fun activities and learn more about science.

www.dkfindout.com/uk/science
Find out more about science and famous scientists.

Comprehension questions

1. What is an experiment?

2. Why is it important for you to ask questions?

Index

24